Common Core Lessons & Activities: Ecosystems

By Carole Marsh

Published by Gallopade International, Inc.

Printed in the U.S.A. (Peachtree City, Georgia)

TABLE OF CONTENTS

G: Includes Graphic Organizer
GO: Graphic Organizer is also available 8½
download at www.gallopade.com/clie
(numbers above correspond to the graphic org

I0895164

What is an Ecosystem?

Read the text and answer the questions.

Take a look outside after a rainstorm, and what do you see? You will most likely find leaves and branches littering your front yard. Puddles have formed. You may even see a tree blown over by the storm. What you may not see is just how the natural balance of the area, or "ecosystem," has changed for the plants and animals living there.

"Ecosystem" is a short name for "ecological system." Ecosystems are found all over the world and there are many types and sizes. They can be as small as a puddle or as large as an ocean. Ecosystems form in deserts, rainforests, and even cold, snowy Antarctica. But, what *exactly* is an ecosystem?

An ecosystem is a community of living things and nonliving things in a specific area. The living things, such as plants and animals, and the nonliving things, such as the soil, water, and climate, are connected by the flow of energy. All living parts of an ecosystem depend on the other parts of the ecosystem to survive.

The balance between plants, animals, and nonliving things is delicate. Take an animal out of an ecosystem, and its predators might not survive. Remove a plant from an ecosystem, and the animals that eat that plant will be affected. Introduce a new plant or animal into an ecosystem, and this may upset the natural balance for the animals and plants already living there.

1. Use the text to define ecosystem.
2. A. What two types of things make up an ecosystem?
   B. Give at least two examples of each.
3. Name three ways all ecosystems are similar to each other.
4. Give three examples of how ecosystems might differ.
5. How does the phrase "natural balance" relate to an ecosystem?
6. Predict how a storm might affect an ecosystem.

Producers

Read the text and answer the questions.

Living things that produce their own food are known as producers. Producers are essential to all ecosystems. Plants, algae, and bacteria are examples of producers.

How do producers produce their own food? They have help from the sun. They do it through photosynthesis. Photosynthesis is the process by which plants capture sunlight and use it to turn carbon dioxide and water into food. The food and energy created by producers feeds and nourishes other living parts of the ecosystem. The process of photosynthesis also creates oxygen, which animals must have in order to breathe!

The flow of energy starts with the sun. Chlorophyll, a substance found inside the cells of leaves, absorbs the sun's energy. The chlorophyll then combines the sun's energy with carbon dioxide (found in the air) and water (brought up through the plant's roots) to make glucose. Glucose is a type of sugar plants use as food—it gives plants energy they need so they can grow. When the plant makes glucose, it releases oxygen into the air.

1. Why are plants considered producers?
2. Why are producers important to an ecosystem?
3. List three things a plant needs for photosynthesis to occur.
4. What two things are created when photosynthesis occurs?
5. Use the text to number the following steps in the correct order.

   _____Chlorophyll absorbs energy from the sun.
   _____The plant uses glucose as energy for growth.
   _____Chlorophyll combines water, carbon dioxide, and the sun's energy to produce glucose.
   _____The sun produces energy.
   _____The plant releases oxygen into the air.
   _____The plant absorbs carbon dioxide from the air and water from the ground.

6. Predict what would happen if photosynthesis stopped happening. List at least three significant effects.

Consumers

Read the text and answer the questions.

Consumers are organisms that get energy and nutrients by eating other organisms.

Consumers can be classified into three types, based on what they eat. Herbivores are animals that eat plants. Herbivores may eat plant roots, seeds, berries, fruit, or any other part of a plant. Herbivores do not eat animals. Carnivores are organisms that eat other animals. Carnivores do not eat plants. Omnivores are organisms that eat both plants and animals.

Consumers can be classified into three levels, based on where they rank on the food chain. A food chain shows the flow of energy between a select group of organisms. Energy flows to an organism on one level when it eats an organism on a different level. The levels on a food chain are called trophic levels. The first trophic level is Producers. The second trophic level is Primary Consumers. Primary Consumers are animals that eat producers. The third trophic level is Secondary Consumers. Secondary Consumers are animals that eat Primary Consumers. In other words, Secondary Consumers eat animals that eat Producers. The fourth trophic level is Tertiary Consumers. Tertiary Consumers are animals that eat Secondary Consumers. A Tertiary Consumer is an animal that eats an animal that eats an animal that eats a producer.

1. Use the text to label the four trophic levels on the diagram. Include each trophic level number and its name.

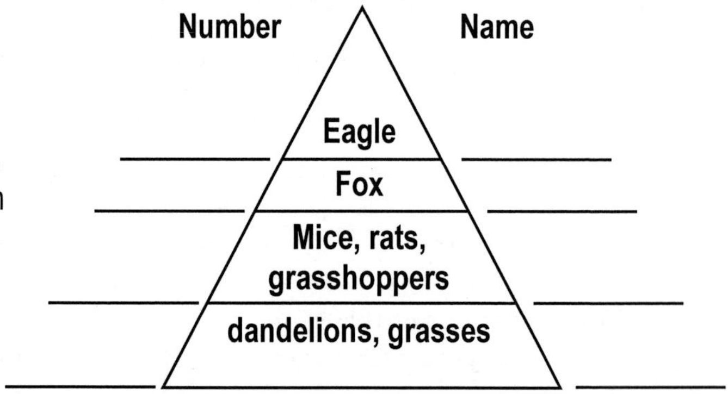

2. Does energy flow up or down on the diagram? Why? Explain your response in a well-organized paragraph.

3. Compare and contrast herbivores, omnivores, and carnivores.

Decomposers

Read the text and answer the questions.

Have you ever wondered why leaves don't just pile up year after year until you can't see the trees anymore? The reason is that after plants and animals die, their remains rot and dissolve. This process of decay is helped along by decomposers.

Decomposers are often called the "recyclers" of life. Decomposers live on decaying matter. Just as consumers eat plants and animals for their energy, organisms like fungi and bacteria get energy from decaying matter. Decomposers produce chemicals to dissolve the dead or decaying matter into nutrients. They then return the nutrient-filled matter to the soil.

The three types of decomposers are fungi, bacteria, and worms. Fungi often grow on stumps or fallen trees. Fungi have a special chemical that breaks down wood. Bacteria, on the other hand, are microscopic so they cannot be seen. They are found everywhere. Bacteria break down decaying matter. Worms are decomposers because they eat decaying matter and their waste becomes nutrients for the soil. A seasoned gardener surely knows that worms are helpful to the plants in his or her garden!

1. A. Use the text to define decomposer.
   B. What purpose do decomposers serve in an ecosystem?
2. Explain why decomposers are called the "recyclers" of life. Cite evidence from the text to support your answer.
3. A. Use the text to define microscopic.
   B. Which type of decomposer is microscopic?
4. Use the text to compare and contrast the three types of decomposers.

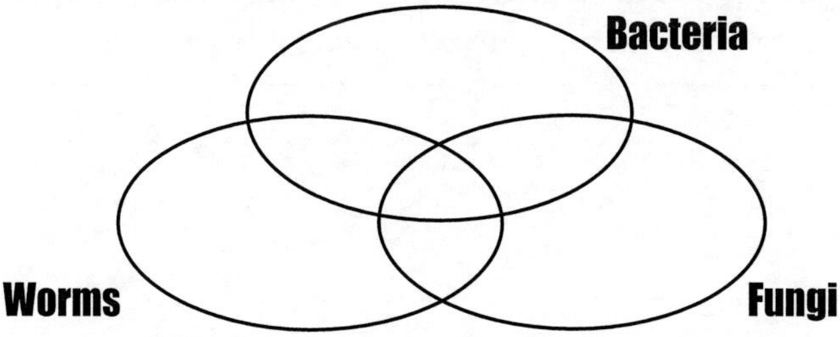

Nonliving Parts of Ecosystems

Read the text and answer the questions.

Ecosystems include nonliving parts such as air, climate, soil, minerals, water, and landforms. These nonliving, or abiotic, parts affect what types of plants and animals live in the ecosystem.

Climate is the weather in an area over a long period of time. Rainfall and air temperature are two aspects of climate. Temperature and rainfall affect the plants and animals that live in an ecosystem. For example, tropical plants grow in rainy climates, not in deserts where they do not get enough water. Similarly, polar bears, with their thick, warm fur, are best-suited to survive in cold arctic climates. Many plants prefer mild temperatures and moderate rainfall. However, plants that grow in hot, desert climates have special abilities to survive the hot sun and lack of rain.

Soil is loose layers of broken-down rock mixed with organic material. Soil may be hard and dry or it may be soft and sandy. Fertile soil, which has plenty of water and nutrients, can sustain many types of plant-life. Loose, rocky soil provides good drainage for many types of trees, while fine silt soil is home to many grasses. Additionally, soil holds minerals that are essential to life.

All plants and animals need water. The movement of water in an ecosystem affects the way of life of many life forms. Still water in lakes and ponds supports a variety of plants and animals. Rain or quickly melting snow can form streams and rivers that nourish many ecosystems. However, water can damage an ecosystem. Flowing water can uproot plants, upsetting the natural balance of an ecosystem. It can also form canyons over time, which may create new ecosystems that support different plant and animal life.

Landforms, such as mountains, hills, valleys, and plains, also affect ecosystems. Mountains tend to be colder and wetter. Their slopes allow for flowing water like streams, but they also lead to erosion. Valleys may create areas of poor drainage, which may be ideal for some plants and animals, but unsuitable for others.

1. Use the text to define <u>abiotic</u>.
2. Use the graphic organizer to identify the four main abiotic factors in the text and to explain the significance of each.

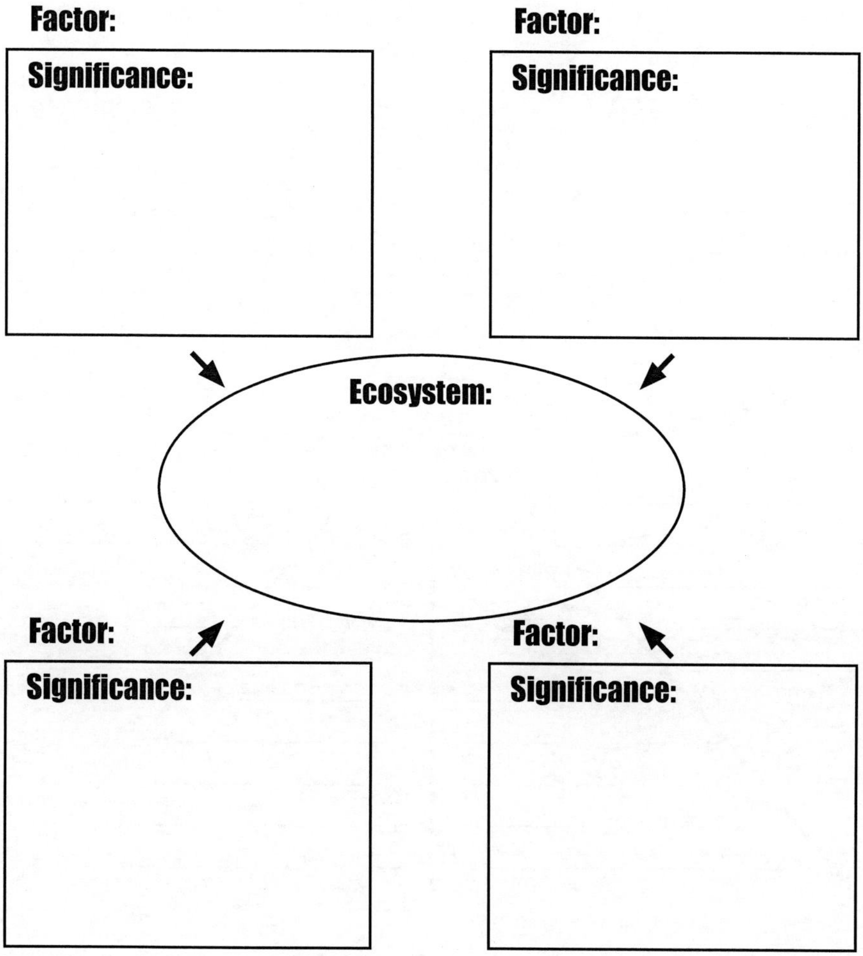

3. A. Give an example of how water can be supportive in an ecosystem.
   B. Give an example of how water can be destructive in an ecosystem.
4. Make three inferences about "unfriendly" ecosystems, such as ecosystems where water is scarce or temperatures are extreme.
5. Give an example of how landform and climate can have an impact on the availability of water in an ecosystem.

MAIN IDEA ORGANIZER

Parts of an Ecosystem

Complete the graphic organizer by explaining the role and significance of each part of an ecosystem. Then answer the questions.

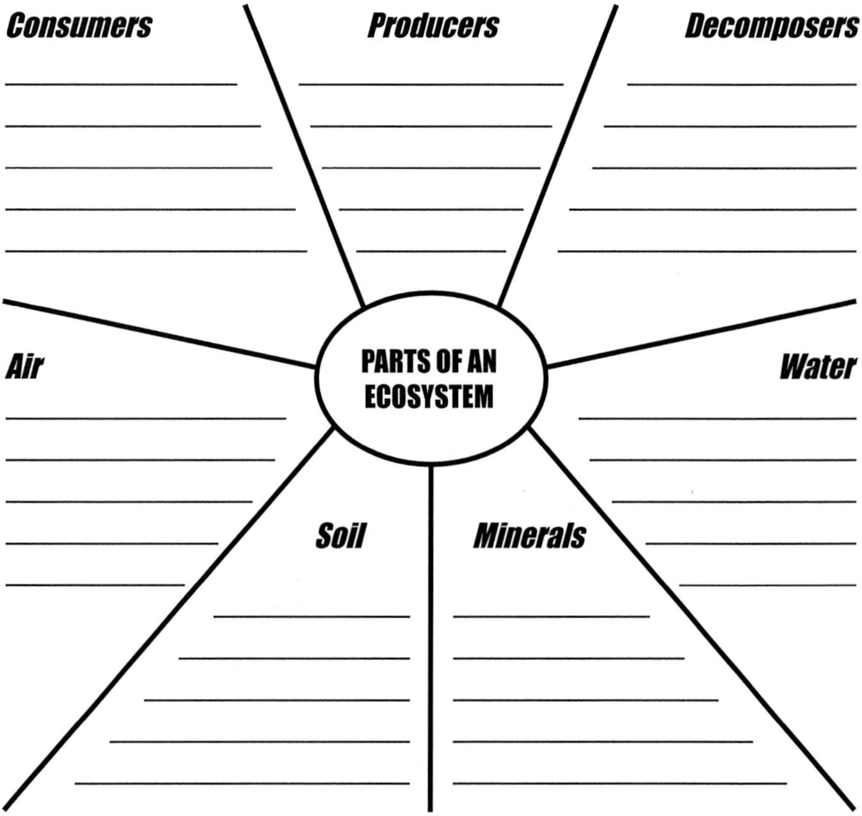

1. From the information you have gathered, write two paragraphs explaining how the nonliving parts of an ecosystem affect the living parts.
2. A. In your opinion, is one part of an ecosystem more important than another? Create a topic sentence to clearly express your opinion, and support your opinion with details and examples from the information you have gathered. Proofread and edit your work.
   B. Share your opinion with the class. How is your opinion similar to that of other students? How is it different?

GRAPHIC ORGANIZER

Flow of Energy

Use your knowledge and online resources to complete the graphic organizer with details about each step in an ecosystem's energy cycle.

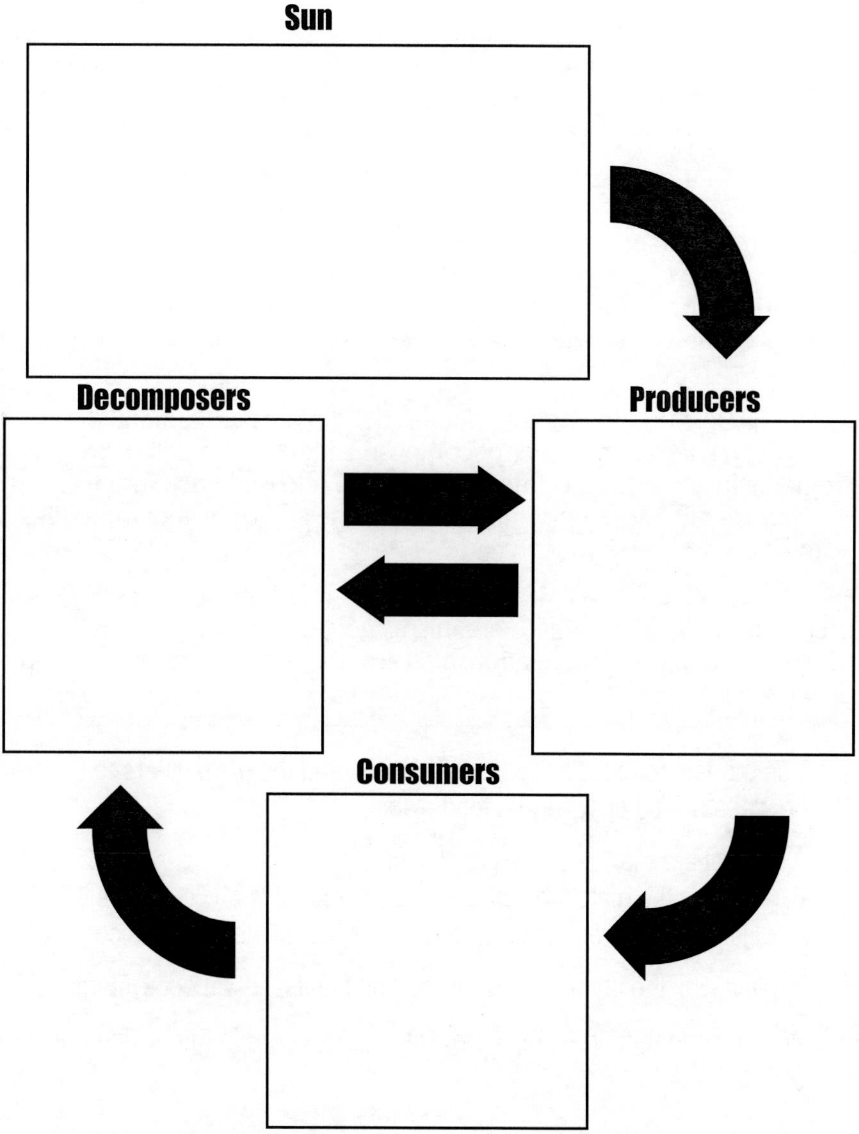

APPLYING CONCEPTS

A Food Web

Read the text and answer the questions.

All living things in an ecosystem are connected by the flow of energy. Unlike a food chain, which shows a single path of energy flow between organisms in a direct path, a food web shows the multi-path flow of energy among organisms in an ecosystem.

The flow of energy starts with the sun. Producers use the sun's energy, as well as water, air, and minerals to make their own food. Plants do this through a chemical process known as photosynthesis. Plants use the food they create as energy to grow.

In contrast, consumers don't produce their own food. They have to get their energy from eating plants or animals. Consumers that only eat plants are called herbivores. Herbivores include squirrels, cows, and deer. Consumers such as foxes and wolves that primarily eat other animals are called carnivores. Consumers that eat both plants and animals are called omnivores.

When plants and animals die, organisms known as decomposers obtain energy from the dead plants and animals. Worms, bacteria, and other decomposers like fungi break down the remains into nutrients or minerals that are released back into the environment. These nutrients end up in the soil or water where they can be reused by producers.

A food web illustrates these various relationships in an ecosystem. It shows where organisms get their food and energy. The more complex the relationships are, the more complex the food web will be!

1. Use the text to explain the main similarity and the main difference between a food chain and a food web.
2. A. What are the three types of consumers?
   B. What is the main difference between producers and consumers?
   C. List at least three things producers and consumers have in common.
3. Explain why the sun is necessary for the survival of an ecosystem.
4. What limited resource helps prevent decomposers from growing out of control? Explain.

Use the text and the information provided in the box labeled "Who Eats Who?" to complete the following steps on the food web diagram:

A. Draw an arrow to show the flow of energy from the sun to the producer. Label the arrow "A."

B. Draw a dashed arrow to show the flow of mineral nutrients to the producer. Label the arrow "B."

C. Draw arrows to show how energy flows to each consumer. Label each of these arrows "C."

D. Draw arrows from every producer and every consumer to show the energy flow that occurs when their remains are decomposed. Label each of these arrows "D."

E. Draw a dashed arrow to show the flow of mineral nutrients to the soil. Label the arrow "E."

Who Eats Who?

- Foxes eat birds, snakes, and squirrels
- Birds eat insects and berries from trees
- Squirrels eat acorns from trees
- Snakes eat squirrels
- Beatles eat leaves from trees
- Worms decompose the remains of dead organisms

GRAPHIC ORGANIZER

Analysis of an Ecosystem

Individually or as part of a small group, choose an ecosystem that you have not already learned about. Ideas include a tidal pool, a marsh, grasslands, a cave, or deep sea. Use classroom and online resources to research the ecosystem. On the graphic organizer, list examples of each part of the ecosystem and describe their significance. Then complete the writing prompt.

Ecosystem:

Producers

Consumers

Decomposers

____

____

____

Nonliving Elements

____

____

____

Threats

____

____

____

Writing Prompt

A. Organize your research into an informative visual such as a poster or digital slideshow. Write accompanying text to explain how each part of the ecosystem is connected.

B. Write a short, first-person narrative to describe what you might see, hear, feel, or taste when visiting your ecosystem. Do not say the name of your ecosystem, but provide informative clues. Proofread and edit your work.

C. Before presenting your visual presentation, read your narrative aloud. Could your audience accurately identify the ecosystem you described? Why or why not?

D. Give your presentation and answer any questions your classmates might have.

Aquatic Ecosystems

An ecosystem in a body of water is known as an "aquatic ecosystem." The two types of aquatic ecosystems are marine ecosystems and freshwater ecosystems. Marine ecosystems are saltwater and they cover approximately 70% of the Earth. Freshwater ecosystems are not saltwater and they include ponds, lakes, streams, and rivers.

Read the text and answer the questions.

A pond is a type of freshwater ecosystem. The living organisms in a pond ecosystem are dependent on and connected with each other as well as with the nonliving parts of the pond ecosystem such as water, minerals, and the sun.

Plants grow in and around the pond. Plants in the pond serve as hiding places for small aquatic animals and fish. Plants around the pond serve as hiding places and homes for birds, turtles, and other animals. Plants are also an important food source for many organisms in the pond ecosystem.

Plankton, small plant and animal organisms that float or drift in the water, are part of a pond's ecosystem. Plankton and algae are a source of food for many organisms at the pond.

Fish, turtles, snakes, frogs, ducks, dragonflies, and birds are examples of some of the animals that live in or around the pond. They are part of the pond ecosystem, too. These animals feed on other plants or animals in or around the pond. They are also the food source for other animals at the pond.

When plants and animals die in the pond ecosystem, decomposers change plant and animal remains into nutrients that help plants grow.

1. List the benefit(s) to the pond ecosystem provided by each of the following:
   A. plants
   B. plankton
   C. producers
   D. consumers
   E. dead plants and animals
2. True or False: An aquatic ecosystem can include plants and animals that do not live in the water.

INFERENCE

Home on the Prairie

The table provides data about some of the prairie ecosystems found in North America.

Look at the table and answer the questions.

	**Tall Grass Prairie** • RAINFALL: 30-40 inches • PLANTS: switch grass, bluestem, wildflowers • ANIMALS: buffalo, antelope, birds • THREATS: agriculture/farming • LOCATION: Midwestern United States
	**Mixed Grass Prairie** • RAINFALL: 10-20 inches • PLANTS: spear grass, june grass • ANIMALS: ground squirrels, burrowing owls, hawks, bison, wolves • THREATS: human development • LOCATION: Central Great Plains
	**Short Grass Prairie** • RAINFALL: 10-15 inches • PLANTS: buffalo grass, cactus, sagebrush • ANIMALS: elk, bison, mule deer • THREATS: highways, fencing, cattle farming • LOCATION: Western Great Plains

1. Identify three characteristics the prairies all have in common based on observations of the photographs.
2. What can you infer about the landforms found in prairies? Explain.
3. Describe the relationship between rainfall and plant growth. Cite evidence from the table to support your answer.
4. In your opinion, what effects do humans have on prairie ecosystems? Cite evidence from the table to support your opinion.

COMPARISON OF PRIMARY SOURCES

Forest Ecosystems

Read the journal entries and answer the questions.

June 8, 2013 I can't help but stare at the thick covering of tall, broad-leafed trees blocking out the sun. This tropical rainforest is so hot and humid! Worms and beetles burrow in the wet earth. Twisted trunks, vines, mosses, and beautiful orchids line the trail. Spiders, lizards, and snakes hide among the leaves. Resting on branches are colorful parrots, toucans, and cuckoos. They take turns entertaining us with their songs. A troop of howler monkeys swing from tree to tree, stopping to eat the abundant fruit. Their loud howl warns other howler monkeys to stay away. A camouflaged sloth hides in a tree above us. Shiny blue and red frogs hop along a stream. Soon we come upon a giant cliff, where a rumbling waterfall crashes below. I am in awe of its power!

October 19, 2013 The autumn air begins to chill me. In a month, snow will fall in this temperate deciduous forest. In the rich soil, mosses, ferns, shrubs, and wildflowers grow. The leaves on the trees have changed to reds and yellows and are beginning to fall. A woodpecker pecks at a tree in the distance. Squirrels scamper up and down trees in search of nuts for winter. A family of white-tailed deer turns to run. We make our way to a lake, where a majestic eagle swoops down and plucks a wriggling fish from the water. She disappears from sight. A red fox takes a drink from the lake, turning to watch us before darting off into the woods.

April 14, 2014 The floor of this evergreen forest is littered with crunchy, fresh-smelling pine needles and spiky pinecones. These pine trees grow close together to keep out the cold. Traces of winter snow lie in the darkest parts of the forest. Spring will soon turn to summer. Few large animals can stand the cold here, but the insect population will rise. Birds that have migrated south to escape the harsh winter will return to feast on the insects. Fresh raccoon tracks appear along the muddy riverbank. From a distance, we watch a snow leopard sunning himself on a wide slab of granite by the river. He takes off in hot pursuit of a gray rabbit. A black bear yawns and ventures toward the river. She spies her next meal and jumps in after it. She must be hungry after her long winter hibernation. It's very possible that she has a few pups in her den. They will need their mother back soon.

1. Summarize details from the text to complete the chart.

Journal Entry: June 8, 2013:	
Type of Forest	
Appearance	
Type of Weather	
Plant Life	
Animal Life	
Interesting Facts	
Journal Entry: October 19, 2013:	
Type of Forest	
Appearance	
Type of Weather	
Plant Life	
Animal Life	
Interesting Facts	
Journal Entry: April 14, 2014:	
Type of Forest	
Appearance	
Type of Weather	
Plant Life	
Animal Life	
Interesting Facts	

2. Analyze the writing style used by the author of the journal entries. For each pairing, choose which word you think best describes the journal entries and cite an example of the text that supports your choice.
   A. formal *-or-* informal
   B. positive *-or-* negative
   C. rich *-or-* bland
   D. concise *-or-* detailed

3. Cite evidence of a food web in each type of forest.

Life in the Desert

Read the text and answer the questions.

You might think of deserts as hot, dry regions with sand and no water in sight. Some deserts look like that, but in fact, most deserts are rocky. Some deserts are even covered in ice, like the Antarctic deserts. Whether it's a sandy desert, an icy desert, or a rocky desert, it probably gets less than 10 inches of rain per year.

Only certain plants and animals are able to live in harsh, dry, desert ecosystems. Often, these plants and animals have special characteristics or adapted behaviors that help them survive.

Desert plant features usually help maximize the use of water. For example, cactus plants have a waxy coating that helps keep in moisture. Desert plants often have shallow root systems so they can collect water when it rains. Some desert plants store carbon dioxide at night, so they can use it for photosynthesis during the day.

Animals in desert ecosystems have adapted unique characteristics to survive, too. In order to save energy, the courser bird runs on the ground instead of flying. An added benefit is he or she can eat insects along the way. One type of desert antelope never has to drink water because it gets liquids from eating plants. Many desert animals, such as coyotes, foxes, and snakes, take shelter during the day and hunt at night when it is cooler.

Even amphibians have adapted to desert life. First they burrow deep in the ground. Then, when rain comes, they leave their burrows and lay eggs in puddles. To survive, the frog eggs must hatch, and the babies must turn from tadpoles to frogs before the water evaporates!

1. What characteristics of a desert ecosystem make survival difficult?
2. Give two examples of features or characteristics that plants or animals in a desert ecosystem have that help them survive. Explain the purpose of each.
3. Give three examples of how plants or animals in a desert ecosystem adapt their behavior to survive. Explain the purpose of each.
4. In your opinion, is it surprising that amphibians are found in deserts? Why or why not?

Human Environments

People design and live in human-made environments that have many similarities to ecosystems. The ecosystem may be small and compact, or it may be large and spread out. It might be crowded, full of life, or sparsely inhabited. It might be flush with resources or resources might be scarce and difficult to find.

Label each of the three photos as urban, suburban, or rural. Then create an analogy for each one and describe how it is like a natural ecosystem. Use your creativity!

All Photos Courtesy of Wikimedia Commons

Threats to an Ecosystem

Individually or in small groups, use the graphic organizer to analyze and propose a solution to one or more of the common threats to ecosystems listed below.

Weather, fire, land development, and many other factors affect ecosystems. Some changes, such as seasons, are natural and help keep an ecosystem in balance. However, some changes may upset the balance of an ecosystem, causing plant and animal life to fail where it once had thrived. Over time, a new balance will be created, and the new ecosystem may be similar—or very different—than the old one.

1. invasive species
2. loss of wildlife
3. habitat loss
4. toxic chemicals
5. loss of resources

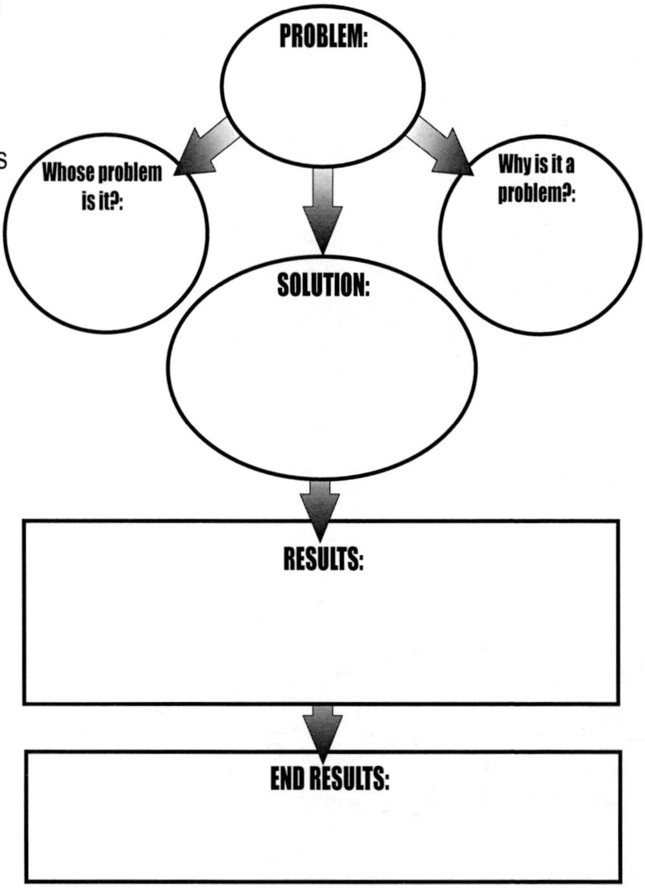

PRIMARY SOURCE ANALYSIS

Ecosystem at Risk

Read the text and look at the photograph. Then answer the questions.

Historically, accidents from oil ships and oil drilling in the ocean have caused significant damage to marine ecosystems. Leaked oil from oil tankers floats on top of the water, sticking to any animal that lives near the ocean's surface. Oil is poisonous to many animals that accidentally digest the oil.

Courtesy of Wikipedia

1. Describe what you see in the photograph by making inferences about who, what, where, and why.
2. What causes oil spills? Cite evidence from the text and photograph.
3. Predict how each of the following might be affected by the oil spill:
   A. ocean birds B. porpoises C. seals D. ocean plants
4. Share your predictions with the class and discuss.
5. What can you infer about the overall effect of an oil spill on a marine ecosystem?

Change over Time: Succession

Read the text and answer the questions.

Over time, everything changes—even ecosystems. Climate change can cause ecosystems to change as well as disturbances such as forest fires, windstorms, flooding, and human activity. For example, a wetland marsh may dry out over time and grow into a forest. Succession is the term we use to describe the change of an ecosystem—plants, animals, and nonliving elements—over time.

Succession might begin with a healthy forest. A disturbance destroys the forest, leaving only an empty field. After awhile, the field begins to grow small flowers and grass. In time, shrubs begin to grow, then small trees. Over more time, shade-loving plants like ferns, moss, and fungi grow underneath the trees. Eventually, larger trees mature into a full forest and the ecosystem becomes stable. Throughout this time, the animal life in the ecosystem is also changing as it goes through succession too.

In all, it may take hundreds of years for full succession to occur. Some scientists say that succession never really stops because something is always disturbing an ecosystem.

1. Use the text to number the pictures in the correct order starting with a healthy forest:

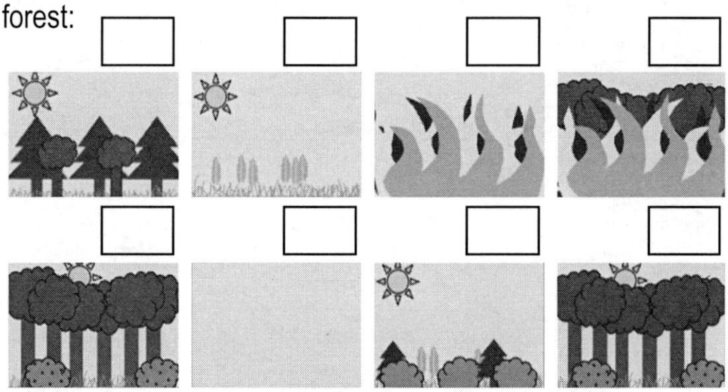

2. A. What disturbance occurred in the succession described?
   B. After the disturbance, what types of plants grew back first?
   C. Explain the relationship between the first and last stages of this succession.

3. Use inferences to list five examples of disturbances that could initiate a significant change to an ecosystem.

Ecosystems Vocabulary

Complete the graphic organizer for each vocabulary word.

adapt
climate
consumer
desert
decomposer
ecosystem
forest
grassland
marsh
photosynthesis
prairie
predator
producer
soil

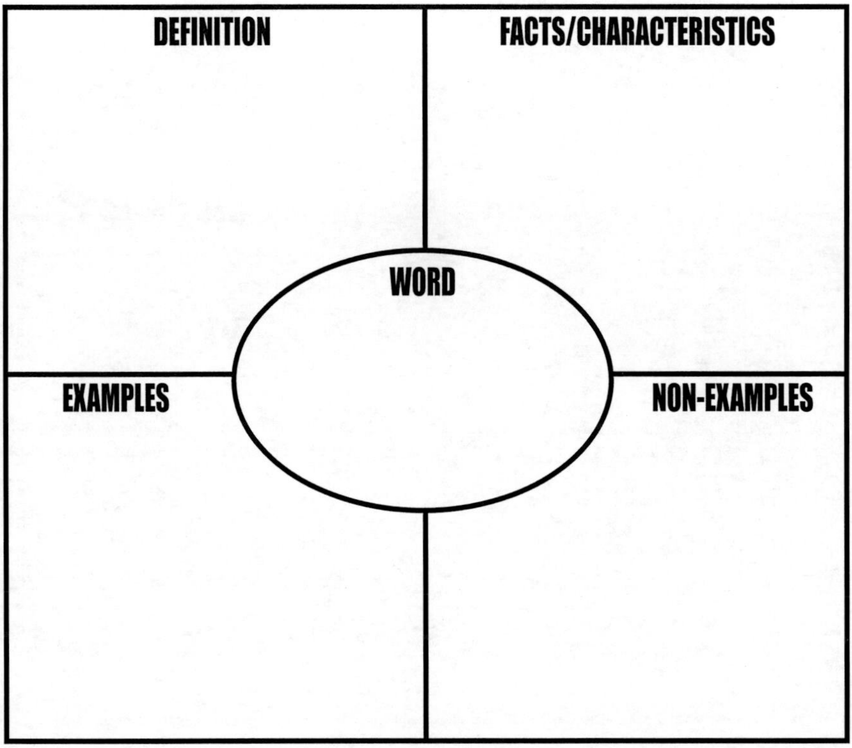

Correlations to Common Core State Standards

For your convenience, correlations are listed page-by-page, and for the entire book!

This book is correlated to the Common Core State Standards for English Language Arts grades 3-8, and to Common Core State Standards for Literacy in History, Science, & Technological Subjects grades 6-8.

Correlations are highlighted in gray.

	READING	WRITING	LANGUAGE	SPEAKING & LISTENING
	Includes: RI: Reading Informational Text; RST: Reading Science & Technical Subjects	*Includes:* W: Writing; WHST: Writing History/Social Studies, Science, & Technical Subjects	*Includes:* L: Language; LF: Language Foundational Skills	*Includes:* SL: Speaking & Listening
PAGE #				
2	RI RST . 1 2 3 4 5 6 7 8 9 10	W WHST . 1 2 3 4 5 6 7 8 9 10	L LF . 1 2 3 4 5 6	SL . 1 2 3 4 5 6
3	RI RST . 1 2 3 4 5 6 7 8 9 10	W WHST . 1 2 3 4 5 6 7 8 9 10	L LF . 1 2 3 4 5 6	SL . 1 2 3 4 5 6
4	RI RST . 1 2 3 4 5 6 7 8 9 10	W WHST . 1 2 3 4 5 6 7 8 9 10	L LF . 1 2 3 4 5 6	SL . 1 2 3 4 5 6
5	RI RST . 1 2 3 4 5 6 7 8 9 10	W WHST . 1 2 3 4 5 6 7 8 9 10	L LF . 1 2 3 4 5 6	SL . 1 2 3 4 5 6
6-7	RI RST . 1 2 3 4 5 6 7 8 9 10	W WHST . 1 2 3 4 5 6 7 8 9 10	L LF . 1 2 3 4 5 6	SL . 1 2 3 4 5 6
8	RI RST . 1 2 3 4 5 6 7 8 9 10	W WHST . 1 2 3 4 5 6 7 8 9 10	L LF . 1 2 3 4 5 6	SL . 1 2 3 4 5 6
9	RI RST . 1 2 3 4 5 6 7 8 9 10	W WHST . 1 2 3 4 5 6 7 8 9 10	L LF . 1 2 3 4 5 6	SL . 1 2 3 4 5 6
10-11	RI RST . 1 2 3 4 5 6 7 8 9 10	W WHST . 1 2 3 4 5 6 7 8 9 10	L LF . 1 2 3 4 5 6	SL . 1 2 3 4 5 6
12-13	RI RST . 1 2 3 4 5 6 7 8 9 10	W WHST . 1 2 3 4 5 6 7 8 9 10	L LF . 1 2 3 4 5 6	SL . 1 2 3 4 5 6
14	RI RST . 1 2 3 4 5 6 7 8 9 10	W WHST . 1 2 3 4 5 6 7 8 9 10	L LF . 1 2 3 4 5 6	SL . 1 2 3 4 5 6
15	RI RST . 1 2 3 4 5 6 7 8 9 10	W WHST . 1 2 3 4 5 6 7 8 9 10	L LF . 1 2 3 4 5 6	SL . 1 2 3 4 5 6
16-17	RI RST . 1 2 3 4 5 6 7 8 9 10	W WHST . 1 2 3 4 5 6 7 8 9 10	L LF . 1 2 3 4 5 6	SL . 1 2 3 4 5 6
18	RI RST . 1 2 3 4 5 6 7 8 9 10	W WHST . 1 2 3 4 5 6 7 8 9 10	L LF . 1 2 3 4 5 6	SL . 1 2 3 4 5 6
19	RI RST . 1 2 3 4 5 6 7 8 9 10	W WHST . 1 2 3 4 5 6 7 8 9 10	L LF . 1 2 3 4 5 6	SL . 1 2 3 4 5 6
20	RI RST . 1 2 3 4 5 6 7 8 9 10	W WHST . 1 2 3 4 5 6 7 8 9 10	L LF . 1 2 3 4 5 6	SL . 1 2 3 4 5 6
21	RI RST . 1 2 3 4 5 6 7 8 9 10	W WHST . 1 2 3 4 5 6 7 8 9 10	L LF . 1 2 3 4 5 6	SL . 1 2 3 4 5 6
22	RI RST . 1 2 3 4 5 6 7 8 9 10	W WHST . 1 2 3 4 5 6 7 8 9 10	L LF . 1 2 3 4 5 6	SL . 1 2 3 4 5 6
23	RI RST . 1 2 3 4 5 6 7 8 9 10	W WHST . 1 2 3 4 5 6 7 8 9 10	L LF . 1 2 3 4 5 6	SL . 1 2 3 4 5 6
COMPLETE BOOK	RI RST . 1 2 3 4 5 6 7 8 9 10	W WHST . 1 2 3 4 5 6 7 8 9 10	L LF . 1 2 3 4 5 6	SL . 1 2 3 4 5 6

For the complete Common Core standard identifier, combine your grade + "." + letter code above + "." + number code above.

In addition to the correlations indicated here, the activities may be adapted or expanded to align to additional standards and to meet the diverse needs of your unique students!